THE COMP___

MICROWAVE

COOKBOOK

Simple, Quick, and Easy Guide with 1000+ Days of Healthy and Delicious Microwave Recipes for Beginners | 21-Day Meal Plan Included

Andrew Fred

Copyright © 2024 by Andrew Fred

CONTENTS

Introduction

Microwave ovens are among the few gadgets that have brought about such a revolutionary change in the way that we prepare food in the world of culinary innovation. To say that the microwave has seen a remarkable metamorphosis is an understatement. From its humble origins as a space-age oddity to its ubiquitous presence in kitchens worldwide, the microwave has undergone a transformation that has altered our views of convenience and efficiency in the kitchen.

The Evolution of Microwave Cooking

During the middle of the 20th century, an engineer named Percy Spencer, who had trained himself to become an engineer, made an unexpected discovery while working with magnetrons, which are the power sources in radar equipment.

This finding led to the development of microwave cooking. Spencer saw that a candy bar in his pocket had melted owing to the microwaves released by the magnetron.

As a result of this fortunate occurrence, the first microwave oven, which was appropriately referred to as the "*Radarange*," was created. This oven was first utilized in industrial settings before it became a home standard.

Since its debut, microwave cooking has expanded to embrace a wide variety of culinary applications, going beyond the traditional functions of reheating and defrosting food.

From baking and steaming to roasting and grilling, the diversity of microwave cooking continues to develop, allowing home cooks limitless opportunities for quick and efficient meal preparation.

Benefits of Microwave Cooking

In addition to being convenient, the advantages of cooking in a microwave go much beyond that.

In today's fast-paced world, when time is of the utmost, the microwave oven appears as a time-saving hero, capable of whipping up tasty meals in a fraction of the time required by conventional cooking methods.

If you are preparing a big breakfast to get your day started or a gourmet dinner to amaze your visitors, the microwave provides an unrivaled level of speed without sacrificing the quality or taste of the food.

Moreover, microwave cooking is recognized for its ability to maintain nutrients in meals, due to its shorter cooking periods and low water usage.

By preserving more vitamins and minerals, microwave-cooked meals contribute to a healthy diet, making it a perfect choice for those seeking nutritious and delectable alternatives to fast food and processed meals.

Understanding Microwave Oven Features

To fully harness the potential of microwave cooking, it's vital to grasp the capabilities and operations of your microwave oven. Each element plays a critical part in obtaining ideal outcomes, from power levels and cooking modes to specialty settings like defrost and sensor cooking.

By mastering these characteristics, you may unleash the whole range of microwave cooking techniques, from delicate steaming to powerful grilling, and adapt your gourmet creations to fit your tastes and preferences.

In this comprehensive cookbook, we dig into the nuances of microwave oven features, giving practical ideas and methods to boost your cooking talents and widen your culinary horizons.

Whether you're a newbie cook trying to expedite meal preparation or a seasoned chef seeking fresh inspiration, this book serves as your necessary guide to mastering the art of microwave cooking.

Join us on a culinary trip filled with tasty dishes, expert advice, and creative techniques as we explore the endless possibilities of microwave cooking. Welcome to "The Comprehensive Microwave Cookbook," where convenience meets creativity in the heart of your kitchen.

Microwave Cooking Basics

Microwave cooking gives us a world of culinary possibilities, giving convenience and efficiency without losing flavor or nutrition. However, to begin this trip with confidence, it's vital to understand the fundamental principles of microwave cooking. In this chapter, we'll study the fundamental factors that build the framework for excellent microwave cooking, from safety warnings to techniques for obtaining properly cooked meals every time.

Safety Precautions

Before going into the domain of microwave cooking, it's vital to emphasize safety. While microwave ovens are constructed with built-in safety mechanisms, following these steps will help prevent mishaps and ensure a smooth cooking experience:

✓ Never activate a microwave oven when it's empty, since it might cause harm to the gadget.

✓ Use microwave-safe containers and utensils to minimize potential risks such as melting or leaching of dangerous chemicals into your food.

✓ When heating liquids, such as soups or beverages, exercise caution to prevent superheating, which can cause abrupt boiling and splattering.

✓ Always observe the manufacturer's guidelines about maximum cooking times and power settings for certain items to prevent overheating or burning.

✓ Avoid heating meals in sealed containers or wrappers, since pressure buildup might cause them to explode.

✓ Take caution while taking hot foods from the microwave, using oven mitts or potholders to protect your hands from burns.

By adhering to these safety measures, you may enjoy the convenience of microwave cooking with peace of mind.

Choosing the Right Microwave-Safe Utensils

Selecting suitable utensils is vital for safe and productive microwave cooking. Here are some suggestions for choosing microwave-safe containers and utensils:

✓ Opt for containers made of glass, ceramic, or microwave-safe plastic for heating or preparing food in the microwave. Avoid containers with metal embellishments, since they might produce sparks and harm to the oven.

✓ Look for containers labeled as "microwave-safe" or with symbols indicating their appropriateness for microwave use. These containers are intended to resist the heat and pressure generated while cooking.

✓ Avoid using containers that are broken, chipped, or bent, since they may not deliver even heating and might pose safety issues.

✓ Use microwave-safe covers or lids to prevent splattering and keep moisture throughout cooking. Avoid closing containers fully, as pressure buildup can develop.

✓ When using tools such as spoons or spatulas, ensure they are made of microwave-safe materials and free from any metal components.

By picking the correct microwave-safe utensils, you can cook with confidence and prevent potential problems in the kitchen.

Understanding Power Levels and Cooking Times

Microwave ovens provide a range of power settings to fit diverse culinary demands, from mild warming to quick frying.

Understanding how to change power levels and cooking times guarantees that your food is cooked evenly and completely. Here's everything you need to know:

- ✓ Microwave ovens often provide numerous power settings, ranging from low to high. Lower power levels are good for delicate foods or chores such as defrosting, while higher power levels are suitable for cooking or reheating.

- ✓ Adjusting the power level allows you to adjust the strength of the microwave energy, minimizing overheating and guaranteeing consistent cooking.

- ✓ When establishing cooking times, consider elements such as the quantity and density of the meal, as well as the desired level of doneness. Start with shorter cooking periods and modify as required to avoid overcooking.

✓ Use microwave-safe covers or microwave-safe plastic wrap to preserve moisture and speed up cooking times for some meals.

✓ For maximum results, rotate or stir food midway through the cooking time to encourage equal heating and prevent hot spots.

By understanding power levels and cooking durations, you may create precisely prepared meals with simplicity and efficiency.

Tips for Even Cooking

Achieving uniform cooking is key to creating delicious and reliable results in the microwave. Follow these techniques to guarantee your food cooks evenly:

✓ Arrange food evenly on the microwave-safe dish, spreading it out in a single layer to facilitate even heating.

- ✓ For heavier meals or recipes with several components, try breaking them into smaller pieces or stacking them in a consistent layer to aid even cooking.

- ✓ Use microwave-safe covers or lids to trap steam and heat, encouraging quicker and more uniform cooking.

- ✓ Stir or rotate food occasionally during the cooking process to disperse heat evenly and prevent hot spots.

- ✓ When preparing dishes with varying textures or densities, modify the cooking times accordingly to ensure that all components are cooked to perfection.

By applying these methods for even cooking, you can boost your microwave culinary talents and prepare tasty dishes with confidence.

Finally, we've built the framework for effective microwave cooking, including basic safety considerations, selecting the correct equipment, understanding power levels and cooking periods, and strategies for ensuring uniform cooking.

Armed with this information, you're ready to begin on a culinary adventure with your microwave oven, discovering new flavors and methods with confidence and inventiveness.

Microwave Cooking Hacks and Tips

Microwave ovens are not just for preparing meals; they can also be immensely beneficial for numerous kitchen hacks and time-saving methods. In this chapter, we'll explore four microwave cooking tricks and methods that will transform the way you approach cooking and meal preparation.

Reviving Stale Bread

There's nothing more frustrating than realizing that your loaf of bread has gone stale. Thankfully, you can simply resuscitate stale bread using your microwave oven:

Instructions

- ✓ Place the stale bread on a microwave-safe dish.

- ✓ Lightly dampen a paper towel and put it over the bread.
- ✓ Microwave on high for 10-20 seconds, depending on the size and thickness of the bread.
- ✓ Check the bread to determine if it has attained the required amount of softness. If not, continue microwaving in 5-second intervals until it's suitably soft.
- ✓ Enjoy freshly softened bread that tastes just like it's fresh from the bakery.

Peeling Garlic Cloves

Peeling garlic cloves may be a difficult and time-consuming operation. However, with this microwave technique, you can peel garlic cloves effortlessly:

Instructions

- ✓ Place the garlic cloves in a microwave-safe basin.
- ✓ Microwave on high for 10-15 seconds.

✓ Remove the bowl from the microwave and allow the garlic cloves to cool slightly.

✓ Once chilled, the garlic cloves should be easy to peel, with the skins falling off readily.

✓ Use the peeled garlic cloves in your favorite recipes, saving time and headaches in the kitchen.

Softening Butter Quickly

Have you ever been in a rush to bake but found that your butter is too hard to deal with? This microwave technique can instantly soften butter to the ideal consistency:

Instructions

✓ Unwrap the stick of butter and set it on a microwave-safe dish.

✓ Microwave on low power for 5-10 seconds, or until the butter begins to melt slightly around the edges.

✓ Rotate the butter and microwave for an additional 5-10 seconds, if required, until it gets the desired softness.

✓ Be cautious not to melt the butter entirely, since it may damage the texture of your baked items.

✓ Use the softened butter in your recipes as needed, saving time and ensuring uniform mixing.

Revitalizing Leftovers

Leftovers are a great way to enjoy excellent meals without the trouble of cooking from scratch. However, warming leftovers in the microwave can occasionally result in uneven heating or mushy textures. Follow these ways to rejuvenate leftovers and guarantee they taste just as wonderful as the day they were made:

Instructions

✓ Place the leftovers in a microwave-safe container with a lid or cover.

✓ Add a dash of water or broth to help rehydrate dry leftovers, such as spaghetti or rice meals.

✓ Microwave on medium power for shorter durations, stirring or turning the meal halfway through, to ensure equal cooking.

✓ Use a microwave-safe cover or lid to trap steam and minimize moisture loss, maintaining the flavor and texture of the leftovers.

✓ Check the temperature of the leftovers with a food thermometer to ensure they reach a safe internal temperature of 165°F (74°C) before serving.

✓ Enjoy revived leftovers that taste just as great as the day they were made, with less work and waste.

By adopting these microwave cooking tricks and ideas into your culinary arsenal, you'll save time, work, and stress in the kitchen while getting excellent results every time.

Experiment with these approaches and learn how your microwave oven can be a flexible tool for increasing your culinary experience.

21-Day Microwave Cookbook Meal Plan

Welcome to the 21-day Microwave Cookbook Meal Plan! In this meal plan, we've organized different tasty and nutritious recipes that can be effortlessly pre-arranged utilizing your microwave. From hearty morning meals to fulfilling dinners and even snacks, every day offers a reasonable determination of feasts to keep you powered and fulfilled.

Whether you're hoping to smooth out your dinner readiness or investigate the accommodation of microwave cooking, this meal plan is intended to assist you with taking advantage of your microwave while getting a charge out of heavenly hand-crafted dinners consistently.

Week 1

Day 1

- ✓ *Breakfast:* Microwave Omelet with Spinach and Feta
- ✓ *Lunch:* Microwave Chicken Caesar Salad with Microwave Croutons
- ✓ *Dinner*: Quick Microwave Bread with Creamy Tomato Soup
- ✓ *Snack*: Microwave Popcorn

Day 2

- ✓ *Breakfast*: Microwave Banana Oats
- ✓ *Lunch:* Microwave Veggie Quesadillas
- ✓ *Dinner:* Microwave Beef Pan fried food with Vegetables
- ✓ *Snack:* Microwave Mug Cake

Day 3

- ✓ *Breakfast:* Microwave Breakfast Burritos

- ✓ *Lunch:* Microwave Chicken Noodle Soup
- ✓ *Dinner:* Microwave Vegetarian Lasagna
- ✓ *Snack*: Microwave Nachos with Salsa

Day 4

- ✓ *Breakfast:* Microwave Blueberry Muffins
- ✓ *Lunch:* Microwave Caprese Salad with Balsamic Glaze
- ✓ *Dinner:* Microwave Fish Filets with Lemon Margarine Sauce
- ✓ *Snack:* Microwave Baked Apples

Day 5

- ✓ *Breakfast:* Microwave Breakfast Sandwiches
- ✓ *Lunch:* Microwave Lentil Soup
- ✓ *Dinner:* Microwave Chicken Alfredo Pasta
- ✓ *Snack:* Microwave Potato Chips with Dip

Day 6

- ✓ *Breakfast:* Microwave French toast
- ✓ *Lunch:* Microwave Stuffed Bell Peppers
- ✓ *Dinner:* Microwave Spaghetti Squash with Marinara Sauce
- ✓ *Snack:* Microwave Apple Crisp

Day 7

- ✓ *Breakfast:* Microwave Greek Yogurt Parfait with Fresh Fruits
- ✓ *Lunch:* Microwave Broccoli and Cheddar Soup
- ✓ *Dinner*: Microwave Beef Bean Chili
- ✓ *Snack*: Microwave Rice Krispie Treats

Week 2

Day 8

- ✓ *Breakfast:* Microwave Egg Muffins with Spinach and Cheese

- ✓ *Lunch:* Microwave Quinoa Salad with Roasted Vegetables
- ✓ *Dinner:* Microwave Teriyaki Chicken with Steamed Rice
- ✓ *Snack:* Microwave Peanut Butter Banana Bites

Day 9

- ✓ *Breakfast:* Microwave Oats Pancakes
- ✓ *Lunch:* Microwave Spinach and Artichoke Dip with Pita Chips
- ✓ *Dinner:* Microwave Vegetable Curry with Basmati Rice
- ✓ *Snack:* Microwave Trail Mix

Day 10

- ✓ *Breakfast:* Microwave Breakfast Quesadillas
- ✓ *Lunch:* Microwave Black Bean Soup
- ✓ *Dinner:* Microwave Shrimp Scampi with Linguine
- ✓ *Snack:* Microwave Veggie Chips

Day 11

- ✓ *Breakfast:* Microwave Berry Smoothie Bowl
- ✓ *Lunch:* Microwave Greek Salad with Homemade Dressing
- ✓ *Dinner:* Microwave Pork Tenderloin with Roasted Potatoes
- ✓ *Snack:* Microwave Cinnamon Sugar Tortilla Chips with Fruit Salsa

Day 12

- ✓ *Breakfast:* Microwave Breakfast Burrito Bowl
- ✓ *Lunch:* Microwave Minestrone Soup
- ✓ *Dinner:* Microwave barbeque Chicken Pizza
- ✓ *Snack:* Microwave Energy Balls

Day 13

- ✓ *Breakfast:* Microwave Banana Bread with Nuts

- ✓ *Lunch:* Microwave Avocado Toast with Poached Eggs
- ✓ *Dinner:* Microwave Meat and Broccoli Sautéed food with Rice Noodles
- ✓ *Snack:* Microwave Veggie Sticks with Hummus

Day 14

- ✓ *Breakfast:* Microwave Chocolate Peanut Butter Oats
- ✓ *Lunch:* Microwave Cobb Salad with Microwave Bacon
- ✓ *Dinner:* Microwave Chicken Teriyaki Bowls with Quinoa
- ✓ *Snack:* Microwave Chessy Garlic Bread Sticks

Week 3

Day 15

- ✓ *Breakfast:* Microwave Breakfast Hash with Eggs

- ✓ *Lunch:* Microwave Taco Salad with Microwave Tortilla Chips
- ✓ *Dinner:* Microwave Beef and Mushroom Stroganoff
- ✓ *Snack:* Microwave Frozen Yogurt Bark

Day 16

- ✓ *Breakfast:* Microwave Breakfast Sandwiches
- ✓ *Lunch:* Microwave Cauliflower Soup
- ✓ *Dinner:* Microwave Lemon Spice Salmon with Asparagus
- ✓ *Snack:* Microwave Granola Bars

Day 17

- ✓ *Breakfast:* Microwave Blueberry Muffins
- ✓ *Lunch:* Microwave Caesar Salad with Microwave Croutons
- ✓ *Dinner:* Microwave Vegan Enchiladas
- ✓ *Snack:* Microwave Caramel Popcorn

Day 18

- ✓ *Breakfast:* Microwave Egg and Cheddar Bagel Sandwiches
- ✓ *Lunch:* Microwave Butternut Squash Soup
- ✓ *Dinner:* Microwave Garlic Butter Shrimp Pasta
- ✓ *Snack:* Microwave Chocolate Mug Cake

Day 19

- ✓ *Breakfast:* Microwave Veggie Omelet
- ✓ *Lunch:* Microwave Kale Salad with Quinoa and Cranberries
- ✓ *Dinner:* Microwave Chicken Parmesan with Spaghetti
- ✓ *Snack:* Microwave Apple Chips

Day 20

- ✓ *Breakfast:* Microwave Banana Pancakes

✓ *Lunch:* Microwave Mediterranean Chickpea Salad
✓ *Dinner:* Microwave Meat Tacos with Microwave Refried Beans
✓ *Snack:* Microwave Rice Pudding

Day 21

Breakfast: Microwave Breakfast Burritos

Lunch: Microwave Thai Nut Noodle Salad

Dinner: Microwave Vegetable Ratatouille

Snack: Microwave Trail Blend Energy Bites

With this 21-day Microwave Cookbook Meal Plan, you'll find the comfort and flexibility of microwave cooking while at the same time partaking in a large number of flavorful dinners and snacks.

Whether you're cooking for yourself or your family, these recipes fulfill your desires and make dinner time a breeze.

Breakfast Delights

A full and tasty breakfast may make all the difference during a hectic morning. In this chapter, we will look at a range of breakfast options that may be simply made in your microwave oven. These dishes will help you start your day off right from fast omelets to warm oatmeal.

Quick Omelettes and Frittatas

Start your day with a protein-rich meal by making a quick omelet or frittata in the microwave. With so many component combinations, you may tailor your omelet or frittata to your taste preferences and nutritional requirements.

Ingredients:

- ✓ Two eggs
- ✓ Two tsp. of milk
- ✓ Salt and pepper to taste.
- ✓ Your preferred fillings (e.g., chopped bell peppers, onions, tomatoes, spinach, ham, bacon, cheese)

Instructions:

1. In a microwave-safe bowl, combine eggs, milk, salt, and pepper.
2. Add your desired fillings, such as diced veggies, cooked meats, cheese, and seasonings.
3. Microwave on high for 2-3 minutes, or until the eggs are set and fully cooked.
4. Let the omelet or frittata cool slightly before slicing and serving.

Preparation time: 5 minutes

Servings: 1

Microwave Pancakes and Waffles

Enjoy fluffy pancakes or crispy waffles without the effort of cooking them on the stove. Homemade breakfast goodies may be ready in minutes thanks to the microwave's ease.

Ingredients:

- ✓ Pancake or waffle mix.
- ✓ Water or milk
- ✓ Toppings of your choice (such as maple syrup, fresh fruit, and whipped cream)

Instructions:

1. In a microwave-safe bowl, blend pancake or waffle mix with water or milk, following package directions.
2. Stir until smooth and well blended.
3. Fill a microwave-safe dish or mug halfway with batter.
4. Microwave on high for 1-2 minutes or until the pancakes or waffles are fully cooked and golden brown.

5. Serve with your preferred toppings, such as maple syrup, fresh fruit, or whipped cream.

Preparation time: 5 minutes

Servings: 1–2.

Breakfast Burritos and Sandwiches

Microwave a breakfast burrito or sandwich for a flavorful and filling breakfast on the run. These protein-rich, flavorful portable breakfasts are ideal for hectic mornings.

Ingredients:

- ✓ Tortilla or English muffin
- ✓ Scrambled eggs.
- ✓ Cooked bacon or sausage
- ✓ Cheese
- ✓ Breakfast toppings of your choosing (e.g., salsa, avocado, chopped tomatoes, spinach)

Instructions:

1. To soften a tortilla or English muffin, microwave them for 10-15 seconds.
2. Fill the tortilla or English muffin with scrambled eggs, cooked bacon or sausage, cheese, and your preferred breakfast toppings.
3. Roll up the tortilla or make the sandwich.
4. Microwave for an additional 30-60 seconds, or until the filling is well cooked and the cheese has melted.
5. Eat your morning burrito or sandwich hot and fresh.

Preparation time: 5 minutes

Servings: 1

Porridge with Oatmeal Variety

Begin the day with a warm and comfortable bowl of porridge or oats. With infinite flavor options, you can tailor your porridge or oatmeal to your taste preferences and nutritional requirements.

Ingredients:

- ✓ Rolled or instant oats
- ✓ Water or milk
- ✓ Toppings of your choosing (such as fresh fruit, nuts, seeds, honey, and cinnamon)

Instructions:

1. In a microwave-safe bowl, mix the oats and water or milk.
2. Microwave on high for 2-3 minutes, stirring halfway through, until the oats are tender and the porridge is creamy.
3. Add your preferred toppings, such as fresh fruit, nuts, seeds, honey, or cinnamon.
4. Stir to mix, then serve hot.

Preparation time: 5 minutes

Servings: 1

With these quick and tasty breakfast options, you'll never miss breakfast again. There's something for everyone, from savory omelets to sweet pancakes, and it's all easy to make in your microwave.

Start your day off properly with these delicious breakfast alternatives.

Appetizer and Snacks

Introducing a delicious selection of appetizers and snacks that can be effortlessly prepared in your microwave oven. From delicious nachos to crispy handmade potato chips, these recipes are ideal for entertaining guests or fulfilling your snack desires. Let's explore the world of microwave treats!

Microwave Nachos and Quesadillas

Prepare to experience the ultimate crowd-pleaser: microwave nachos and quesadillas. These cheesy pleasures are easy to prepare and full of flavor, making them ideal for movie nights or informal parties.

Ingredients:

- ✓ Tortilla chips
- ✓ Shredded cheese (like cheddar or Monterey Jack)
- ✓ Black beans
- ✓ Diced tomatoes.
- ✓ Sliced jalapeno
- ✓ Optional toppings include chopped onions, black olives, and cooked minced beef or chicken.

Instructions

1. Spread a layer of tortilla chips onto a microwave-safe dish.
2. Top the chips with shredded cheese, beans, chopped tomatoes, jalapenos, and any other preferred toppings.
3. Microwave on high for 1-2 minutes, or until the cheese melts and bubbles.
4. Serve hot with salsa, guacamole, and sour cream to dip.

Preparation time: 5 minutes

Servings: 2-4.

Homemade Potato Chips and Popcorn

Enjoy the crispy pleasure of homemade potato chips and popcorn prepared directly in the microwave. With only a few basic ingredients, you can enjoy these traditional treats without the guilt of store-bought alternatives.

Ingredients:

- ✓ Potatoes
- ✓ Season with salt, pepper, and an optional seasoning mix.
- ✓ Popcorn Kernels
- ✓ Butter (Optional)

Instructions:

1. Thinly slice potatoes using a mandoline or knife.
2. Arrange the potato slices in a single layer on a microwave-safe dish, taking care not to overlap.
3. Microwave on high for 3-5 minutes, or until the chips turn golden and crispy, checking and turning halfway through.

4. Season with salt and pepper or your preferred seasoning combination.

5. To make popcorn, pour 1/4 cup kernels into a microwave-safe dish and cover with a plate.

6. Microwave on high for 2-3 minutes, or until the popping slows to 2-3 seconds for each pop.

7. Season with melted butter and salt, if preferred.

Preparation time: 10 minutes

Servings: varies

Stuffed Mushrooms with Jalapeno Poppers

Improve your appetizer game with microwave-made stuffed mushrooms and jalapeño poppers. These bite-sized snacks are ideal for gatherings or as a delicious snack at any time of day.

Ingredients:

✓ Mushrooms

- ✓ Jalapenos
- ✓ Cream Cheese
- ✓ Shredded cheese
- ✓ Cooked bacon or sausage is optional.
- ✓ Breadcrumbs
- ✓ Herbs (like parsley and chives)

Instructions:

1. Remove the stems from the mushrooms and jalapenos, then scrape out the seeds and membranes.
2. Fill each mushroom cap with a combination of cream cheese, herbs, and breadcrumbs.
3. Fill the jalapenos with a mixture of cream cheese, shredded cheese, and cooked bacon or sausage.
4. Put the filled mushrooms and jalapenos in a microwave-safe dish.
5. Microwave on high for 3–5 minutes, or until the filling is heated and bubbling.
6. Serve hot and relish the flavorful goodness.

Preparation time: 15 minutes

Servings: varies

Dips and Salsas

An appetizer dish is incomplete without a variety of dips and salsas. These versatile condiments, ranging from creamy avocado dip to fiery tomato salsa, bring flavor and excitement to any snack tray.

Ingredients:

- ✓ Ripe avocados
- ✓ Lime juice
- ✓ Garlic
- ✓ Diced tomatoes.
- ✓ Onions
- ✓ Jalapenos
- ✓ Cilantro
- ✓ Shredded cheese
- ✓ Milk
- ✓ Spices (e.g., chili powder, cumin, paprika).

Instructions:

1. Make avocado dip by mashing ripe avocados with lime juice, garlic, salt, and pepper until smooth.

2. To make tomato salsa, add chopped tomatoes, onions, jalapenos, cilantro, lime juice, salt, and pepper in a basin.

3. In a microwave-safe dish, combine shredded cheese, milk, and seasonings. Stir until smooth and creamy.

4. Serve the dips and salsas alongside chips, crackers, or vegetable crudites for dipping.

Preparation time: 10 minutes

Servings: varies.

With these delicious appetizers and snacks, you'll be able to amaze your visitors or have a gratifying treat at any time of day.

There's something for everyone, from creamy nachos to crunchy potato chips, and it's all easy to make in the microwave.

Soups and Salads

Soups and salads are adaptable meals that provide the ideal blend of flavor, nutrition, and comfort. In this chapter, we will look at a variety of delicious soups and salads that may be simply made in your microwave oven. From creamy classics to vivid salads, these dishes will fulfill your desires while also nourishing your body.

Creamy Tomato Soup

Ingredients:

- ✓ Two cans (14 ounces each) of Diced tomatoes
- ✓ One onion, diced
- ✓ Two cloves of garlic, minced
- ✓ Two cups of veggie broth.
- ✓ Half a cup of heavy cream.
- ✓ Season with salt and pepper to taste.
- ✓ Garnish with fresh basil leaves.

Instructions:

1. In a microwave-safe bowl, mix the diced tomatoes, onion, and garlic.

2. Microwave the onions on high for 5 minutes, or until tender and transparent.

3. Carefully transfer the contents to a blender and process until smooth.

4. Return the combined mixture to the microwave-safe bowl, then whisk in the veggie broth and heavy cream.

5. Microwave on high for a further 3-4 minutes, or until well cooked.

6. Season with salt and pepper to taste.

7. Ladle the soup into bowls and top with fresh basil leaves before serving.

Preparation time: 10 minutes

Servings: 4

Chicken Noodle Soup

Ingredients:

- ✓ Two cups of cooked chicken, shredded.
- ✓ Four cups of chicken broth
- ✓ One carrot, sliced
- ✓ One celery stalk, sliced
- ✓ Half onion, chopped
- ✓ One cup of uncooked egg noodles.
- ✓ Add salt and pepper to taste.
- ✓ Fresh parsley for garnish.

Instructions:

1. In a microwave-safe dish, mix the shredded chicken, chicken broth, carrot, celery, and onion.
2. Microwave on high for 8 to 10 minutes, or until the veggies are soft.
3. Stir in the uncooked egg noodles and microwave for an additional 5-6 minutes, or until well cooked.
4. Season with salt and pepper to taste.
5. Ladle the soup into bowls and top with fresh parsley before serving.

Preparation time: 15 minutes

Servings: 4

Caesar Salad with Microwave Croutons

Ingredients:

- ✓ One head of romaine lettuce, chopped
- ✓ Half a cup of Caesar dressing.
- ✓ One-quarter of a cup of grated parmesan cheese.
- ✓ Two slices of bread, cubed
- ✓ Two tbsp. of olive oil.
- ✓ Half a tsp. of garlic powder.
- ✓ Add salt and pepper to taste.

Instructions:

1. In a large mixing basin, combine the chopped romaine lettuce and Caesar dressing until equally covered.

2. Toss the salad with grated Parmesan cheese.

4. In a separate microwave-safe dish, combine the cubed bread, olive oil, garlic powder, salt, and pepper.
5. Microwave the bread cubes on high for 2-3 minutes, or until brown and crispy. Stir halfway through.
6. Allow the croutons to cool slightly before mixing them into the salad.
7. Serve the Caesar salad with microwave croutons right away for a crisp and tasty variation on a classic favorite.

Preparation time: 5 minutes

Servings: 2.

Spinach and Quinoa Salad

Ingredients:

- ✓ One cup of quinoa, cooked
- ✓ Two cups of baby spinach leaves.
- ✓ Half a cup of cherry tomatoes (halved)

- ✓ One-quarter cup of sliced almonds.
- ✓ One-quarter cup of crumbled feta cheese.
- ✓ Two tbsp. of balsamic vinaigrette.
- ✓ Add salt and pepper to taste.

Instructions:

1. In a large mixing bowl, add cooked quinoa, baby spinach leaves, cherry tomatoes, sliced almonds, and crumbled feta cheese.
2. Pour the balsamic vinaigrette over the salad and toss to coat evenly.
3. Season with salt and pepper to taste.
4. Serve the spinach and quinoa salad immediately for a healthful and delightful dinner.

Preparation time: 15 minutes

Servings: 4

In this chapter, we looked at a range of soups and salads that may be simply made in your microwave oven. Whether you want a hearty cup of soup or a vivid salad filled with flavor, these dishes will satisfy your taste buds and feed your body.

Main Courses

Welcome to the core of the meal, the main dish. In this chapter, we'll look at a variety of major dishes that are not only delicious but also easy to make in your microwave oven. From velvety pasta to sizzling stir-fry, these dishes will enhance your dining experience without requiring hours in the kitchen. Let's take a look at some tasty main meals you can make in your microwave.

Chicken Alfredo Pasta

Indulge in the rich and creamy tastes of chicken Alfredo pasta, a traditional Italian meal that will please the entire family. With the convenience of your microwave, you can have this cozy dinner ready in no time.

Ingredients:

- ✓ Eight ounces of fettuccine pasta
- ✓ One cup of cooked chicken breast strips.
- ✓ One cup of Alfredo sauce.
- ✓ Freshly grated Parmesan cheese, for garnish.
- ✓ Chopped parsley for garnish.

Instructions:

1. Cook the pasta according to package directions until al dente.
2. In a microwave-safe bowl, mix the cooked chicken breast strips and Alfredo sauce.
3. Microwave the chicken on high for 2-3 minutes, or until well cooked.
4. Stir in the cooked pasta until thoroughly coated with the sauce.
5. Serve hot, topped with freshly grated Parmesan and chopped parsley.

Preparation time: 15 minutes

Servings: 2-3.

Beef Stir-Fry with Vegetables

Savor the powerful flavors of beef stir-fry with veggies, a quick and filling supper ideal for busy weeknights. With your microwave's high heat, you can get delicate steak and crisp-tender veggies in minutes.

Ingredients:

- ✓ Eight ounces of beef sirloin, thinly sliced
- ✓ Two cups mixed veggies (such as bell peppers, broccoli, and carrots), thinly sliced
- ✓ Two tbsp. of soy sauce.
- ✓ Two cloves of garlic, minced
- ✓ One tsp. of grated ginger.
- ✓ Cooked rice or noodles, for serving.

Instructions:

1. Thinly slice beef against the grain and marinade in soy sauce, garlic, and ginger.
2. Stir fry marinated beef and cut veggies in a microwave-safe bowl until well done.

3. Microwave on high for 5-6 minutes, stirring halfway through, or until the meat is browned and the veggies are soft and crispy.
4. Serve hot with prepared rice or noodles.

Preparation time: 20 minutes

Servings: 2-3.

Fish Fillets with Lemon Butter Sauce

Treat yourself to delicate and flaky fish fillets in a zesty lemon butter sauce, a light and elegant main meal suitable for any occasion. With the mild heat of your microwave, you can have properly cooked fish in minutes.

Ingredients:

- ✓ Two fish fillets (like tilapia or salmon)
- ✓ Two tbsp. of butter, melted
- ✓ One tbsp. of lemon juice.
- ✓ Add salt and pepper to taste.
- ✓ Chopped parsley for garnish.

✓ Lemon slices for garnish.

Instructions:

1. Put the fish fillets in a microwave-safe dish and sprinkle with melted butter and lemon juice.
2. Season with salt, pepper, and any herbs of your preference.
3. Microwave on medium-high for 5-6 minutes, or until the fish is opaque and readily flaked with a fork.
4. Serve hot, topped with lemon slices and chopped parsley.

Preparation time: 10 minutes

Servings: 2

Vegetarian Lasagna

Enjoy the layers of flavor in this substantial vegetarian lasagna, which is loaded with veggies, cheese, and rich marinara sauce.

With the convenience of your microwave, you can enjoy this warm dish without the need for a lengthy baking time.

Ingredients:

- ✓ Six lasagna noodles were prepared according to the package
- ✓ Two cups of marinara sauce.
- ✓ One cup of ricotta cheese.
- ✓ One cup of chopped spinach.
- ✓ One cup of shredded mozzarella cheese.

Instructions:

1. In a microwave-safe dish, combine lasagna noodles, marinara sauce, ricotta cheese, spinach, and shredded mozzarella.

2. Repeat layers until all ingredients are utilized, finishing with a layer of marinara sauce and shredded mozzarella on top.

3. Microwave on high for 8-10 minutes, or until the lasagna is fully cooked and the cheese is melted and bubbling.

4. Allow a few minutes for the lasagna to set before serving.

Preparation time: 20 minutes

Servings: 2-3.

With these delectable main dishes, you can have restaurant-quality dinners in the comfort of your own home. From Italian-inspired pasta recipes to Asian-inspired stir-fries, there's something for everyone's taste, and it's all easy to make in the microwave.

Enjoy convenience without compromising taste!

Side Dishes

Welcome to the side dishes part of your microwave cookbook, where we'll look at four delightful accompaniments for your main entrée. From creamy mashed potatoes to savory rice pilaf, these side dishes are tasty and simple to make in your microwave oven. Let's explore the world of tempting sides that can enrich any dinner.

Garlic Mashed Potatoes

These mashed potatoes are creamy, buttery, and imbued with a powerful garlic taste, making them the ideal side dish for any dinner. With the convenience of a microwave oven, you can quickly prepare this classic comfort dish.

Ingredients:

- ✓ Four big peeled and diced potatoes
- ✓ Two minced garlic cloves
- ✓ Two tbsp. of butter
- ✓ One-quarter cup milk
- ✓ Salt and pepper to taste
- ✓ Chopped parsley as garnish

Instructions:

1. Peel and dice potatoes into cubes. Place in a microwave-safe basin.
2. Cover potatoes with water and microwave on high for 8-10 minutes, or until cooked.
3. Drain potatoes and return to bowl.
4. Combine the potatoes with butter, garlic, milk, salt, and pepper.
5. Mash potatoes until smooth and creamy. Add additional milk if needed.
6. Garnish with parsley if preferred, and serve hot.

Preparation time: 15 minutes

Servings: 4

Steam Vegetables with Herbs

These steamed veggies with herbs are a beautiful, flavorful, and healthful side dish. With the gentle steam from your microwave, you can maintain the natural tastes and nutrients of the veggies while infusing them with fragrant herbs.

Ingredients:

- ✓ Two cups chopped mixed veggies (e.g. broccoli, carrots, and cauliflower).
- ✓ Dried herbs, including thyme, rosemary, and Italian seasoning.
- ✓ Add salt and pepper to taste.

Instructions:

1. Combine mixed veggies (e.g. broccoli, carrots, cauliflower) in a microwave-safe dish.
2. Top with water and dried herbs (e.g., thyme, rosemary, or Italian seasoning).
3. Cover the dish with a microwave-safe cover or plastic wrap, leaving a tiny vent to let steam out.
4. Microwave on high for 4-6 minutes, or until veggies are soft and crisp.

5. Season with salt and pepper to taste.

6. Serve hot as a colorful and healthy side dish.

Preparation time: 10 minutes

Servings: 2-3.

Rice Pilaf with Mixed Nuts

Improve your rice game with this aromatic and savory pilaf sprinkled with crunchy mixed nuts. With the help of your microwave oven, you can prepare flawlessly cooked rice laced with aromatic spices and roasted almonds.

Ingredients

- ✓ One cup of long-grain rice
- ✓ Two cups water
- ✓ Two tbsp. of butter
- ✓ One-quarter cup chopped onion
- ✓ Spices (cumin, coriander, turmeric)
- ✓ Mixed nuts (almonds, cashews, and pistachios)

Instructions:

1. In a microwave-safe dish, mix rice, water, butter, chopped onion, and desired spices (e.g. cumin, coriander, turmeric).

2. Cover the dish with a microwave-safe cover or plastic wrap, leaving a tiny vent to let steam out.

3. Microwave on high for 12-15 minutes until rice is cooked and fluffy.

4. Fluff rice with a fork and add mixed nuts (almonds, cashews, and pistachios).

5. Serve hot as a tasty and filling side dish.

Preparation time: 20 minutes

Servings: 4

Creamy Macaroni with Cheese

Creamy, creamy, and irresistibly cozy, this macaroni and cheese is the ideal side dish for any dinner.

With the convenience of a microwave oven, you can quickly prepare this classic comfort dish.

Ingredients:

- ✓ Two cups of elbow macaroni
- ✓ One cup of milk
- ✓ Two cups shredded cheese (either cheddar or mozzarella)
- ✓ Two tsp. of butter
- ✓ Salt and pepper to taste.

Instructions:

1. Cook macaroni according to package directions until al dente.
2. In a microwave-safe dish, mix cooked macaroni, milk, cheese, and butter.
3. Microwave on high for 2-3 minutes until cheese melts and sauce is creamy, stirring halfway through.
4. Season with salt and pepper according to taste.
5. Serve hot as a warm and pleasant side dish.

Preparation time: 15 minutes

Servings: 4

With these tasty side dishes, you can improve any dinner with ease. From creamy mashed potatoes to savory rice pilaf, these dishes will add variety and flavor to your meal.

Enjoy the convenience of microwave cooking while maintaining taste and quality!

Desserts

Indulge your sweet taste with a delicious assortment of desserts that can be effortlessly prepared in your microwave oven. From rich and indulgent chocolate lava cake to soothing bread pudding, these dishes will fulfill your desires while wowing your visitors. Let's dive into the realm of microwave treats that will have you coming back for more.

Molten chocolate lava cake

Enjoy the ultimate chocolate lover's treat with this delectable molten chocolate lava cake. With a gooey chocolate core that seeps out with each bite, this delicacy is sheer delight.

Ingredients:

- ✓ Two ounces of dark chocolate, chopped.
- ✓ Two tbsp. of unsalted butter.
- ✓ One-quarter cup of granulated sugar.

- ✓ One huge egg.
- ✓ Two tbsp. of all-purpose flour.
- ✓ One tsp. of cocoa powder.
- ✓ Powdered sugar or vanilla ice cream for garnish.

Instructions:

1. In a microwave-safe dish, heat the butter and chocolate in short bursts, stirring until smooth.
2. Stir in the sugar, eggs, flour, and cocoa powder until well blended.
3. Divide the batter equally into microwave-safe ramekins.
4. Microwave on high for 45-60 seconds, or until the borders are firm but the middle remains somewhat mushy.
5. Let it cool for a minute before serving.
6. If desired, sprinkle with powdered sugar or top with a dollop of vanilla ice cream.

Preparation time: 10 minutes

Servings: 2.

Berry Crisp with Oat Topping.

Enjoy the taste of summer with this delectable berry crisp topped with crispy oats. You can quickly prepare this fruity treat using your microwave.

Ingredients:

- ✓ Two cups of mixed berries (including strawberries, blueberries, and raspberries)
- ✓ Two tsp. of granulated sugar.
- ✓ One tbsp. of cornstarch.
- ✓ Half of a cup of old-fashioned oatmeal
- ✓ One-quarter cup of all-purpose flour.
- ✓ Half a cup of brown sugar.
- ✓ Half a tsp. of crushed cinnamon
- ✓ Two tbsp. of unsalted butter, melted
- ✓ Whipped cream or vanilla yogurt, for serving.

Instructions:

1. In a microwave-safe dish, combine the berries, sugar, and cornstarch.
2. In a separate dish, combine the oatmeal, flour, brown sugar, cinnamon, and melted butter until crumbly.

3. Distribute the oat topping evenly over the fruit mixture.

4. Microwave on high for 5-7 minutes, or until the berries bubble and the topping turns golden brown.

5. Let it cool for a few minutes before serving.

6. Serve warm, with a dollop of whipped cream or vanilla yogurt.

Preparation time: 15 minutes

Servings: 2-3

Bread Pudding with Caramel Sauce

This warm, soothing, and wonderfully delicious bread pudding with caramel sauce is the ideal dessert for a night in. With the convenience of your microwave, you can enjoy this classic comfort dish without having to bake it for hours.

Ingredients:

- ✓ Two cups of cubed bread.
- ✓ One cup of milk.

6. Microwave on high for 8-10 minutes, or until the bread feels firm to the touch and a toothpick inserted into the center comes out clean.

7. Let the banana bread cool slightly before slicing and serving.

Preparation time: 15 minutes

Servings: 1 loaf.

Blueberry Muffins

Ingredients:

- ✓ Two cups of all-purpose flour.
- ✓ Half a cup of granulated sugar.
- ✓ One tbsp. of baking powder.
- ✓ Half a tsp. of salt
- ✓ One cup of milk.
- ✓ One-quarter of a cup of vegetable oil.
- ✓ One egg, beaten
- ✓ One tsp. of vanilla essence.
- ✓ One cup of blueberries, fresh or frozen.

Instructions:

1. In a large mixing basin, combine all-purpose flour, granulated sugar, baking powder, and salt.

2. In a separate dish, mix the milk, vegetable oil, beaten egg, and vanilla essence.

3. Gradually mix the wet and dry ingredients, stirring until just blended.

4. Gently fold in the blueberries.

5. Fill microwave-safe muffin cups about two-thirds full with batter.

6. Microwave on high for 3-4 minutes for each batch, or until the muffins feel firm to the touch and a toothpick inserted into the center comes out clean.

7. Allow the muffins to cool somewhat before taking them out of the muffin tins and serving.

Preparation time: 20 minutes

Servings: 12 muffins

Chocolate Chip Cookies

Ingredients:

- ✓ Half a cup of unsalted butter softened.
- ✓ Half a cup of granulated sugar.
- ✓ One-quarter of a cup packed brown sugar.
- ✓ One egg
- ✓ One tsp. of vanilla extract
- ✓ One-quarter of a cup of all-purpose flour.
- ✓ Half a teaspoon of baking soda.
- ✓ One-quarter of a teaspoon of salt.
- ✓ Half a cup of semisweet chocolate chips.

Instructions:

1. In a large mixing bowl, combine the softened butter, granulated sugar, and brown sugar. Beat until light and fluffy.

2. Beat in the egg and vanilla essence until thoroughly mixed.

3. In a separate basin, combine all-purpose flour, baking soda, and salt.

4. Gradually add the dry ingredients to the butter mixture, stirring just until incorporated.
5. Fold in the semi-sweet chocolate chips.
6. Place rounded portions of dough on a microwave-safe plate, spaced approximately 2 inches apart.
7. Microwave on high for 1-2 minutes, or until the cookies are firm and brown on the edges.
8. Allow the cookies to cool briefly before moving them to a wire rack to cool entirely.

Preparation time: 15 minutes

Servings: 12 cookies.

In this chapter, we looked at a range of baking and bread recipes that may be simply done in your microwave oven. Whether you want a freshly baked loaf of bread, moist banana bread, fluffy blueberry muffins, or chewy chocolate chip cookies, these recipes will fulfill your sweet and savory desires with little time and effort.

Beverages

Welcome to the beverage part of your microwave cookbook, where we will look at a range of warming and delicious beverages that may be quickly prepared in your microwave oven. From warm mulled cider to decadent hot chocolate, these recipes are ideal for snuggling up on cold evenings or taking a peaceful afternoon break. Let us explore the world of microwaveable beverages that will tempt your taste buds and warm your spirit.

Mulled Cider

Enjoy the aromas of the season with this fragrant and spicy mulled cider. This warming beverage is ideal for Christmas gatherings or pleasant nights by the fire, and it will bring warmth and happiness into your house.

Ingredients:

- ✓ Four glasses of apple cider.
- ✓ Two cinnamon sticks.
- ✓ Six whole cloves.
- ✓ Two orange slices.

Instructions:

1. In a microwave-safe container, mix the apple cider, cinnamon sticks, cloves, and orange slices.
2. Microwave on high for 3-4 minutes, or until the cider is well-cooked and flavored with spices.
3. Allow to steep for a few minutes so that the flavors can combine.
4. Transfer the mulled cider to cups and serve hot.
5. Garnish with a cinnamon stick or an orange slice if preferred.

Preparation time: 5 minutes

Servings: 4

Hot Chocolate

Indulge in a thick, creamy cup of hot chocolate, a timeless favorite that will warm you from the inside out. This delectable dessert can be prepared in minutes using your microwave.

Ingredients:

- ✓ One cup of milk.
- ✓ Two tbsp. of unsweetened cocoa powder.
- ✓ One-to-two tsp. of sugar, to taste.
- ✓ Pinch of salt.
- ✓ Half a tsp. of vanilla essence.
- ✓ Whipped cream or marshmallows for topping.

Instructions:

1. In a microwave-safe cup, mix the milk, cocoa powder, sugar, and a sprinkle of salt.
2. Microwave on high for 1-2 minutes, or until the milk is heated but not boiling, stirring halfway through.
3. Stir in the vanilla extract until well-mixed.
4. Top with whipped cream or marshmallows, if preferred.

5. Serve hot and enjoy the comforting warmth of handmade hot chocolate.

Preparation time: 5 minutes

Servings: 1

Herbal Teas

Relax and unwind with a cup of herbal tea flavored with aromatic herbs and spices. With the convenience of your microwave, you may enjoy a range of herbal teas according to your tastes.

Ingredients:

- ✓ Herbal teabag or loose tea leaves
- ✓ Hot water
- ✓ Sweeten with honey or agave syrup (optional).

Instructions:

1. Put your favorite herbal tea bag or loose tea leaves in a microwave-safe cup.
2. Fill the mug with boiling water, about 3/4 full.

3. Microwave on high for 1-2 minutes, or until the tea is the appropriate strength.

4. Remove the teabag or sieve the tea leaves.

5. Sweeten with honey or agave syrup if preferred.

6. Serve hot and enjoy the soothing benefits of herbal tea.

Preparation time: 3 minutes

Servings: 1

Microwave Coffee Creations

These inventive and tasty microwave coffee inventions will elevate your coffee experience. From flavorful lattes to foamy cappuccinos, these recipes will elevate your daily coffee experience.

Ingredients

- ✓ Strong brewed coffee.
- ✓ Milk-flavored syrups, including vanilla and caramel.
- ✓ Sprinkle with cocoa powder or cinnamon for garnish.

Instructions:

1. Make a strong cup of coffee with your preferred beans or instant coffee powder.
2. Froth milk with a whisk or a microwave-safe frother.
3. Place the coffee in a microwave-safe mug and heat on high for 30-60 seconds, or until hot.
4. If desired, stir in flavored syrups like vanilla or caramel.
5. Finish with frothed milk and a sprinkling of chocolate powder or cinnamon.
6. Serve hot and enjoy your great handmade coffee.

Preparation time: 5 minutes

Servings: 1

With these delicious beverage recipes, you can easily enjoy a range of warm and pleasant drinks. From spicy mulled cider to velvety hot chocolate, there is something for every taste and occasion.

Healthy and Quick Meals

In this chapter, we will look at a variety of nutritious and time-saving meals that you can quickly make in your microwave oven. From colorful veggie bowls to protein-rich fish plates, these recipes are intended to fuel your body without compromising flavor or convenience. Let's explore the world of nutritious and quick meals that will keep you satiated and energized all day.

Vegetable-Packed Quinoa Bowl

Fuel your body with a flavorful and nutrient-dense quinoa meal. This nutritious meal, which is high in protein, fiber, and important minerals, is ideal for busy days when you need something quick and satisfying.

Ingredients

- ✓ One cup of quinoa, rinsed
- ✓ Two cups water or veggie broth.
- ✓ Assorted veggies (bell peppers, cherry tomatoes, cucumbers, and avocado)
- ✓ Cooked chickpeas or tofu are optional.
- ✓ Dressing or sauce of your choosing

Instructions:

1. Rinse the quinoa under cold water before placing it in a microwave-safe bowl with water or broth.
2. Microwave on high for 6-8 minutes, or until the quinoa is tender and fluffy.
3. Meanwhile, cut up your favorite vegetables (such as bell peppers, cherry tomatoes, cucumbers, and avocado).
4. When the quinoa is done, fluff it with a fork and divide it into serving dishes.
5. Top the quinoa with chopped veggies, cooked chickpeas or tofu, and a drizzle of your preferred dressing or sauce.

6. Serve hot or cold, and savor a nutritious and tasty meal.

Preparation time: 15 minutes

Servings: 2.

Microwave-Steamed Fish and Vegetables

Enjoy a light and healthy dinner of microwave-steamed salmon with veggies, which are high in protein, vitamins, and minerals. Your microwave's gentle steam can cook succulent fish and crisp-tender veggies in minutes.

Ingredients:

✓ Two fish fillets (like tilapia or salmon)
✓ Assorted veggies (carrots, broccoli, and bell peppers)
✓ Salt and pepper to taste.
✓ Drizzle with olive oil or lemon juice.

Instructions:

1. Place the fish fillets in a microwave-safe dish and season with salt, pepper, and your preferred herbs or spices.
2. Arrange sliced veggies (such as carrots, broccoli, and bell peppers) around the fish.
3. Drizzle with olive oil or lemon juice for extra taste.
4. Cover the dish with a microwave-safe cover or plastic wrap, leaving a tiny opening for steam to escape.
5. Microwave on high for 5-6 minutes, or until the fish is opaque and easily flaked with a fork, and the veggies are soft and crisp.
6. Serve hot, with a squeeze of lemon juice and a sprinkling of fresh herbs.

Preparation time: 10 minutes

Servings: 2.

Microwave Eggplant Parmesan

Enjoy the taste of classic Italian food with this microwave eggplant Parmesan, a healthier version of the traditional dish.

This recipe, with soft eggplant slices topped with marinara sauce and melted mozzarella, is likely to become a favorite.

Ingredients

- ✓ One big sliced eggplant with Marinara sauce.
- ✓ Shredded mozzarella cheese.
- ✓ Chopped fresh basil or parsley for garnish.

Instructions

1. Slice the eggplant into 1/4-inch thick rounds and place in a microwave-safe dish.
2. Microwave the eggplant on high for 3-4 minutes, or until soft.
3. Spread marinara sauce over the eggplant pieces and top with shredded mozzarella.
4. Repeat the layers until all of the eggplant slices are used up.

5. Microwave on high for another 2-3 minutes, or until the cheese is melted and bubbling.

6. Serve hot and garnish with chopped fresh basil or parsley.

Preparation time: 10 minutes

Servings: 2.

Greek Yogurt Parfait with Fresh Fruits

Start your day on a healthy note with this Greek yogurt parfait, topped with fresh fruit and crunchy granola. This nutritious breakfast alternative, which contains protein, probiotics, and fiber, will keep you full and energized until midday.

Ingredients:

- ✓ Greek yogurt
- ✓ Various fresh fruits (strawberries, blueberries, bananas)
- ✓ Granola

✓ Drizzle with honey or maple syrup.

Instructions:

1. Warm a little quantity of honey or maple syrup in a microwave-safe bowl for a few seconds until it is easy to drizzle.
2. In serving glasses or bowls, combine Greek yogurt, cut fresh fruits (such as strawberries, blueberries, and bananas), and granola.
3. Drizzle honey or maple syrup over top for extra sweetness.
4. Repeat the layering until the glasses are filled to your satisfaction.
5. Serve immediately for a refreshing and nutritious breakfast.

Preparation time: 5 minutes

Servings: 2.

With these healthy and quick meal ideas, you can fuel your body with complete foods without spending hours in the kitchen. From colorful quinoa bowls to protein-rich fish meals, these recipes are ideal for hectic days when you need a nutritious lunch quickly.

Enjoy the convenience without sacrificing flavor or nutrients!

Conclusion

In this voyage into the world of microwave cooking, we've looked at the convenience, variety, and limitless possibilities that this basic kitchen equipment provides. From quick and easy dinners to rich desserts, the microwave has proven to be a great tool for culinary discovery and innovation. As we near the finish of this cookbook, let's consider three crucial characteristics that have impacted our culinary experience:

Accepting the Convenience of Microwave Cooking

The microwave oven has transformed the way we cook and eat, providing a quick and economical way to prepare meals while preserving taste and nutrients. With its fast heating and perfect temperature control, the microwave has become an invaluable tool in modern kitchens.

By adopting microwave cooking, we may save time, energy, and effort while still eating excellent cooked meals.

Experimenting and Customizing Recipes

One of the most enjoyable aspects of cooking is the freedom to experiment with ingredients, tastes, and techniques to create one-of-a-kind dishes. There are unlimited choices when it comes to microwave cooking.

Whether you're modifying old recipes to suit your tastes or creating new meals from scratch, don't be scared to be creative in the kitchen. Use the microwave as a canvas and let your creativity run wild.

Final Thoughts and Encouragement for Culinary Exploration

As we wrap up this cookbook, I want to urge you to continue exploring the world of microwave cooking with curiosity and passion. Try new recipes, experiment with various ingredients, and don't be afraid to make errors along the way.

Cooking is a journey of discovery, and each meal you prepare provides a chance to learn and improve as a home chef.

So, let us continue to enjoy the process of cooking and cherish the great flavors and memories we make together.

In conclusion, I want to thank you for accompanying me on this gastronomic trip. I hope this cookbook has encouraged you to be creative in the kitchen and explore the limitless possibilities of microwave cooking.

Remember that the enjoyment of cooking stems not only from the finished product but also from the process of production. So, keep cooking, researching, and, most importantly, enjoying the delightful flavors of home-cooked meals.

Happy cooking!

- ✓ Two eggs
- ✓ One-quarter cup of granulated sugar.
- ✓ One tsp. of vanilla essence.
- ✓ Half a tsp. of crushed cinnamon
- ✓ Store-bought caramel sauce
- ✓ Cinnamon or whipped cream as garnish

Instructions:

1. In a microwave-safe dish, mix the cubed bread, milk, eggs, sugar, vanilla essence, and cinnamon.
2. Microwave on medium power for 6-8 minutes, stirring halfway through, or until the bread pudding has set and the bread is completely saturated.
3. In a separate microwave-safe dish, heat store-bought caramel sauce until it's warm and pourable.
4. Serve the bread pudding warm and drizzled with caramel sauce.
5. If desired, garnish with cinnamon or whipped cream.

Preparation time: 15 minutes

Servings: 2-3.

Microwave Cheesecake with Fruit Topping

Enjoy a creamy and luscious cheesecake topped with fresh fruit for a refreshing and delicious dessert. With the convenience of your microwave, you can enjoy homemade cheesecake without the need for a water bath or a lengthy baking period.

Ingredients:

- ✓ Eight ounces of cream cheese softened
- ✓ Half a cup of granulated sugar.
- ✓ One-quarter of a cup of sour cream.
- ✓ One tbsp. of lemon juice.
- ✓ One tsp. of vanilla essence.
- ✓ Two eggs, beaten
- ✓ Fresh fruit for topping (strawberries, blueberries, raspberries)

Instructions:

1. In a microwave-safe bowl, combine the cream cheese, sugar, sour cream, lemon juice, and vanilla extract until smooth.

2. Add the beaten eggs and stir until well blended.

3. Transfer the cheesecake batter to a microwave-safe dish lined with parchment paper.

4. Microwave on medium power for 10-12 minutes, or until the cheesecake is firm around the edges but somewhat jiggly in the center.

5. Allow it to cool fully before chilling in the refrigerator for at least 2 hours.

6. Before serving, garnish with your favorite fresh fruit (strawberries, blueberries, or raspberries).

Preparation time: 20 minutes

Servings: 6-8

With these delectable treats, you can fulfill your sweet tooth in no time. There's something for everyone, from rich chocolate lava cake to fresh berry crisp, and it's all easy to make in your microwave oven.

Baking & Bread

B aking in a microwave oven may appear strange to some, but it's a quick and easy method to make wonderful bread and baked goods. In this chapter, we'll look at a range of delicious dishes, from speedy microwave bread to rich chocolate chip cookies, all of which are simple to make in your microwave oven.

Quick Microwave Bread

Ingredients:

- ✓ Two cups of all-purpose flour.
- ✓ One tbsp. of baking powder.
- ✓ One tsp. of salt.
- ✓ One cup of milk.
- ✓ Two tbsp. of vegetable oil.

Instructions:

1. In a large mixing basin, combine all-purpose flour, baking powder, and salt.

2. Gradually add the milk and vegetable oil until a smooth batter develops.

3. Pour the batter into a loaf pan that is microwave-safe and has been gently oiled or coated with parchment paper.

4. Microwave on high for 6-8 minutes, or until the bread feels firm to the touch and a toothpick inserted in the center comes out clean.

5. Let the bread cool slightly before slicing and serving.

Preparation time: 10 minutes

Servings: 1 loaf

Banana Bread with Nuts

Ingredients:

✓ Two ripe bananas, mashed

- ✓ One-third of a cup of melted butter.
- ✓ Three-quarters of a cup of granulated sugar.
- ✓ One egg, beaten
- ✓ One tsp. of vanilla essence.
- ✓ One and a half cups of all-purpose flour.
- ✓ One tsp. of baking soda.
- ✓ Half a tsp. of salt.
- ✓ Half a cup of chopped nuts (walnuts or pecans)

Instructions:

1. In a large mixing basin, add mashed bananas, melted butter, granulated sugar, beaten egg, and vanilla essence.
2. In a separate basin, combine all-purpose flour, baking soda, and salt.
3. Gradually add the dry ingredients to the banana mixture, stirring just until incorporated.
4. Fold in the chopped nuts.
5. Pour the batter into a loaf pan that is microwave-safe and has been gently oiled or coated with parchment paper.